RYA National Windsurfing Scheme Syllabus & Logbook

© RYA

Third Edition 2019
Reprinted January 2020

The Royal Yachting Association
RYA House, Ensign Way,
Hamble, Southampton,
Hampshire SO31 4YA

Tel: 02380 604 100
Web: www.rya.org.uk
Follow us on Twitter @RYAPublications or on YouTube

We welcome feedback on our publications at publications@rya.org.uk

You can check content updates for RYA publications at www.rya.org.uk/go/bookschangelog

ISBN 978-1-910017289
RYA Order Code G47

Sustainable Forests

Cover design: Pete Galvin
Photographic credits: Minorca Sailing, Neilson, Sam Ross, Mark Warner, Paul Wyeth, Tony Wyeth
Typeset: creativebyte
Proofreading: Matthew Gale
Printed in China through World Print

Contents

4   The RYA National Windsurfing Scheme

5   Find the Right Windsurfing Course

7   RYA Windsurfing Syllabus

9   The Duke of Edinburgh's Award

10   Introduction to the National Scheme Coaching

12   Start Windsurfing
An introduction to the sport – getting you up and sailing around

14   Intermediate Windsurfing: Non-planing
Slicker turns, improved stance, and an introduction to the harness

17   Intermediate Windsurfing: Planing
Sailing in stronger winds and using the footstraps

20   Intermediate Windsurfing: Clinics
Specific clinics concentrating on beachstarting and gybing the board

22   Advanced Windsurfing
Improve your sailing skills in a variety of conditions and equipment

25   Advanced Windsurfing: Clinics
Everything an open-water sailor needs to know about waterstarting
and the famous carve gybe; progressing on to advanced carving skills
and confidence building in bump and jump conditions and getting air

29   RYA WINDFoiling Course
The three-level RYA WINDFoiling course will get you flying fast

35   RYA Racing Course
With three levels, the Racing Syllabus takes you from being a
complete beginner to a competent racer

42   Becoming an Instructor

44   What's Next?

45   Personal Log

47   Certificates

The RYA National Windsurfing Scheme

Windsurfing offers something for everyone, as it is an addictive sport for all ages and abilities. The RYA Scheme has been designed to help you progress rapidly through the sport, whether you are looking to cruise around a lake or learn to jump off waves.

The Scheme incorporates an incredibly effective and memorable coaching system, focusing on enhancing your progression throughout all aspects of the sport.

The RYA National Windsurfing Scheme acknowledges the need to provide training to suit all participants in a simple and flexible manner. The fantastic advances in equipment encourage speedy progression towards a competent ability.

Welcome to windsurfing and happy sailing!

Amanda Van Santen
Chief Instructor, Dinghy & Windsurfing

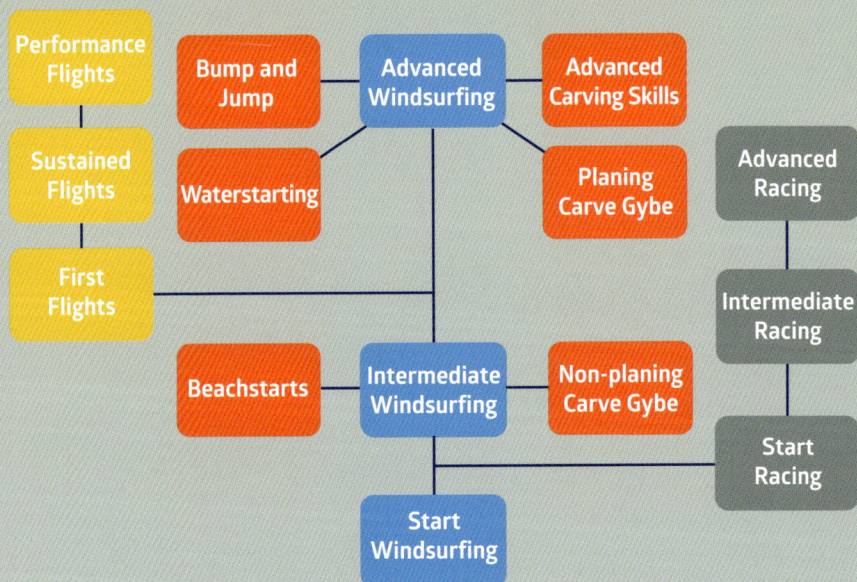

- Performance Flights
- Sustained Flights
- First Flights

- Bump and Jump
- Advanced Windsurfing
- Advanced Carving Skills
- Waterstarting
- Planing Carve Gybe
- Advanced Racing
- Beachstarts
- Intermediate Windsurfing
- Non-planing Carve Gybe
- Intermediate Racing
- Start Racing
- Start Windsurfing

Find the Right Windsurfing Course

The RYA National Schemes have been developed to help you progress rapidly through the sport, whatever your age or level of ability.

Like any activity, good tuition and sound advice mean that you will learn efficiently, and more importantly, ensure you'll enjoy all that windsurfing has to offer.

To select a course that will meet your needs, use the RYA website's 'Where's My Nearest?' feature for a list of windsurfing schools near you.

YOUR COURSE

Throughout the RYA National Windsurfing Scheme you will be taken progressively through the skills needed to become a competent sailor in a variety of conditions. Each level has criteria enabling you to log your progression and set yourself goals, and enhance your knowledge and understanding of the environment we sail in and the mechanics of the sport. In addition to the practical elements, each section covers a small amount of sailing background.

To enable you to choose the right course, the RYA National Windsurfing Scheme has been designed so that, depending on your prior experience, you can find a starting level that suits you. All that's left to do now is to find the course best suited to you.

RYA NATIONAL WINDSURFING SCHEME

Start Windsurfing
A first introduction to the sport. This teaches you the basics so you are up and sailing around in as little as eight hours. There are no prerequisites to this course other than a degree of water confidence.

Intermediate Windsurfing
The unique Fastfwd coaching system your Instructor uses will form the backbone to your progression throughout windsurfing. Within this course you will get to grips with the harness, footstraps, and more dynamic skills in stronger winds. Beachstarting and gybing are taught either as a clinic or combined in a course tailored to an individual's needs and the teaching environment.

Advanced Windsurfing
Advanced windsurfing is all about blasting control and tacking in varying water states. Broken down and coached using the Fastfwd formula, aided by the use of a variety of equipment, many of the elements of the course can be learnt and practised in lighter winds. Waterstarting and carve gybing, along with other advanced modules, can be taught as part of a course, clinic, or as an ongoing learning experience.

Windfoiling Courses

If harness and footstraps brought a feeling of exhilaration, wait until you try foiling! On completing the RYA Intermediate Course you will have the skills required to give foiling a go and experience the thrill and excitement of windsurfing above the water.

RYA Racing Courses

The RYA Racing course has three levels: Start, Intermediate, and Advanced. Having completed your Start Windsurfing Course, you'll be at the right level to begin the Start Racing Course. As you get better, you can progress until you have done your Advanced level, by which time you will be giving some of the best national racers a run for their money!

With a network of local clubs to help introduce you to the fun of racing, you may want to take one step further and progress to achieve your true potential.

RYA Windsurfing Syllabus

RYA RECOGNISED TRAINING CENTRES

There are about 220 RYA Training Centres around the UK and overseas that deliver the National Windsurfing Scheme. Safety is the RYA's priority; all our centres are inspected annually to ensure high standards of instruction, equipment, facilities, and safety. RYA recognition enables centres to use the RYA tick mark logo to promote their courses. Always look for the logo when deciding where to take your course. An RYA Training Centre should display a Certificate of Recognition specifying the activities for which they are recognised. With all windsurfing courses there should be no more than six students to every Instructor.

On completing your course, the Principal or Chief Instructor of the centre will decide whether certificates are to be awarded. They may decide that further practice is necessary before awarding you a certificate. If this is the case, they will explain the reasons to you. If you are unhappy with the way your course has been run, or wish to appeal against the outcome, you may contact RYA Training for guidance.

THE SCHEME

Throughout the RYA Windsurfing Scheme syllabus there are three competency levels to show you in how much depth you can expect each practical or theoretical item to be covered.

Has knowledge of the subject:
The subject will be briefly explained. Familiarisation occurs during the course and information is provided on where to find out more.

Understands the subject:
The subject will be covered in greater depth. You will be asked to demonstrate a basic understanding, and leave the course able to further develop your own skills in this area.

Can demonstrate a level of proficiency in the subject:
Background theory and practical demonstrations will be covered in greater depth by the Instructor and through repeated practice by yourself until you can demonstrate good skills in this subject.

Logging your Course
To log your progression, individual items can be signed off by your assessing Instructor, or, once you have successfully completed a level, your logbook will be signed and dated by the Principal or Chief Instructor.

Experienced sailors may wish to have a direct assessment of their skills rather than taking part in a training course. The criteria are outlined for each level in the appropriate sections of the logbook.

How to Become an Instructor

Having learnt to sail, you may enjoy passing your skills on to others. The RYA Instructor is an experienced windsurfer who has successfully completed a windsurfing test (the pre-entry test) and an Instructor training course. Further information is on the RYA website and on pages 42–43 of this book.

RYA Instructors should also hold a first aid certificate and the RYA Powerboat Level 2 Certificate. Full details are contained in RYA publication W33, RYA Windsurfing Instructor Manual.

Courses for Young People

The RYA also offers a training scheme for young people, the Youth Windsurfing Scheme. Full details are published in RYA book W1. Following completion of the Youth Windsurfing Scheme, young people may participate in further training through the advanced modules of the National Windsurfing Scheme.

Learning Resources

The RYA produces a wide range of materials to help you learn, from handbooks to online courses. These can be obtained through RYA Training Centres and the RYA website.

The Duke of Edinburgh's Award

ARE YOU AGED BETWEEN 14 AND 24 AND FANCY CHALLENGING YOURSELF?

The RYA is recognised as a National Operating Authority for The Duke of Edinburgh's Award (DofE). The DofE is a voluntary, non-competitive programme of activities for anyone aged 14 to 24, providing a fantastic opportunity to experience new activities or develop existing skills.

There are three progressive levels of programmes that, when successfully completed, lead to a Bronze, Silver, or Gold Award.

SAILING AS PART OF YOUR DofE

Achieving a DofE Award can be made an adventure from beginning to end. Within an RYA club or training centre there are already many activities you could take part in that can count towards your DofE. These could range from:

Volunteering
Helping out at your local training centre, club, or Team15 night on a regular basis. This could be as an assistant, in the kitchen, or maybe even on the committee!

Physical
Regularly taking part in sailing or windsurfing activity? Why not set yourself a goal to gain a certain certificate in the RYA National Sailing or Windsurfing Scheme, or maybe participate in regular club racing?

Skill
Develop your skills, whether practical, social, or personal. You may choose to sharpen up your powerboating, learn a new skill such as boat repair work, become an Instructor, or perhaps increase your theory knowledge and learn all about meteorology!

Residential and Expedition
You may never have been away from home before, let alone used your board or boat to go on an exciting adventure with friends, so now is the time!

Further information can be found, explaining the opportunities available, on the DofE website (www.dofe.org), and the RYA website (www.rya.org.uk/go/dofe).

Introduction to the National Scheme Coaching

FAST*FWD*

In recent years we have seen a variety of user-friendly equipment designs that now offer the perfect platform to relish the sport. In conjunction with this recent equipment evolution, windsurfing skills and coaching techniques have also seen massive advances.

Fast*fwd* Coaching

To take full advantage of these exciting changes, RYA Windsurfing turned to technique expert Simon Bornhoft. Simon was particularly keen to simplify and focus on the exact skills, techniques, and coaching methods that really do make a difference on the water and stay with you right throughout the sport.

No matter the level of windsurfer, we all stand on a board with our hands and feet roughly shoulder-width apart as we cruise along. From this position, our aim is to control the equipment in the conditions and enjoy the great thrill of windsurfing. If you look at a very experienced windsurfer blasting along, they aren't actually doing anything wildly different to the less experienced sailor. What separates them is the ability to focus on and commit to a small number of simple, yet very specific, techniques. In truth, there are no magical secrets and no complex actions to master. It's all about getting better at the basics.

Fast*fwd* fuses the fundamental principles of the sport into a unique, easily applied, and memorable Formula. The Formula contains five key elements that are supported by some specific actions and techniques, all of which are an integral part of everything we do on a board and are totally transferable into every area of the sport.

The Fast*fwd* Formula has proven to be a very simple, memorable, and incredibly versatile coaching method for all levels. Sometimes we focus heavily on one of the five elements, but often it is the combination of all the elements that provides the catalyst for progression. Fast*fwd* is a simple common language between you and your Instructor which can also act as a self-coaching tool.

Because the Formula relates to both planing and non-planing environments across all levels, it forms the basis of virtually everything we do on a board.

VISION	TRIM	BALANCE	POWER	STANCE
Where you look, your sailing line, and how you use your head	A flat, stable platform increases the ease with which we can control the board and rig in any situation	OR counterbalance refers to our continuous objective of maintaining our distance from the rig, and always opposing and counterbalancing the rig's pull, position, and movement with our body	Power refers to channelling the rig's drive	Stance refers to how we use our body to best effect while we are sailing

Start Windsurfing

This is the first course in the RYA Windsurfing Scheme. There are no prerequisites to Start Windsurfing other than a degree of water confidence.

It is a gentle introduction to the sport of windsurfing, teaching you the basics so you can turn the board around, sail to where you want to go, and get back to shore. With a bit of practice following this course, you will soon start to feel very comfortable in as little as eight hours afloat.

PRACTICAL

Rigging, Launching, Starting and Landing
- Understands basic rigging and de-rigging
- Has knowledge of the names and the uses of the main components of the board and rig

Has practical understanding of:
- Carrying and launching board and rig
- Getting on the board, using uphaul for balance
- Lifting the rig out of the water, establishing the secure position
- Lowering the rig, coming ashore, and positioning equipment safely
- A basic method of self-rescue

S4   Signature

Sailing Techniques, Stance, and Manoeuvres

Has practical understanding of the following manoeuvres:
- Static steering: progressing on to turning through 180 degrees, either nose or tail through the wind

- The sailing position and sailing across the wind
- Controlling power in the rig
- Stopping
- Steering on the move, understanding the relationship between the Centre of Effort and Centre of Lateral Resistance
- Tacking on the move to change direction, understanding the main points of sailing
- Sailing upwind, understanding the 'no go zone' and its effect on the means of sailing upwind
- Sailing downwind
- Gybing on the move to change direction

S4   Signature

Can:
- Make progression upwind and downwind, understanding when to tack and gybe.
- Understand the terms windward; leeward; upwind; downwind; port; starboard

S4   Signature

Sailing Conditions, Safety, and Equipment

Understands the basic principles of:

The seven common senses:

1. Is all your equipment seaworthy and suitable?

2. Tell someone where you are going and when you will be back

3. Obtain a forecast for the local sailing area

4. Are you capable of handling prevailing conditions?

5. Sail with others

6. Avoid strong tides, offshore winds, and poor visibility

7. Consider other water users

- Basic rules of the road – power gives way to sail, port versus starboard, overtaking vessel, windward vessel

- Basic equipment: boards and rigs – size and suitability

Su

Signature

ASSESSMENT CRITERIA

The students' knowledge and ability will be assessed on a continual basis in winds over three knots. Having satisfactorily completed all sections, the students should be awarded an RYA Start Windsurfing Certificate and also introduced to the Intermediate Course and regular participation opportunities.

Sk

Signature

Intermediate Windsurfing: Non-planing

The Intermediate Course is split into two competencies and further clinics to encourage smooth progression. At many RYA centres the course will be combined as the core skills are transferable. Your prior ability and weather conditions will have relevance as to the level of assessment throughout the course. The aim of this level is simply to enhance techniques. You will use the Fastfwd Formula to make launching slicker, turns faster, slip into the harness, and adapt your stance to cope with more power. If you've already been hooked by the freedom and exhilaration of windsurfing, just wait until the wind gets up! It is assumed that any student on this course has mastered the practical skills and background knowledge required for the Start Windsurfing Course.

NON-PLANING CRITERIA

Launching, Starting and Landing
Can:

- Carry and launch the board and rig together

- Use improved uphauling

- Stop under control

- Return to shore safely

- Remove from the water and leave the board and rig together securely on the shore

Signature

Sailing Techniques, Stance and Manoeuvres
Within this section the student should build a basic practical knowledge and apply the Fastfwd Formula to enhance their sailing ('Vision, Trim, Balance, Power and Stance').

Has practical understanding of the following:

- Improved stance on all points of sailing

- Gust control

- Maintaining sailing line

- Improved steering using body weight and the rig

- Sail adjustment on all points of sailing

- Intro to the harness and basic harness technique

Signature

Can:

- Sail with competence on all points of sail, with and without the daggerboard (understanding uses and limitations)

- Tack – with better use of the rig and weight control

Signature

SAILING BACKGROUND

Rigging
Has an understanding of:

- Choosing and rigging a sail suitable for the prevailing conditions

- Basic sail tuning

- Parts of a sail

Signature

Rescue Techniques and Safety
Has an understanding of:
- The importance of self-help and self-rescue
- Safety equipment and essential spares
- Awareness of other water users

Signature

Sailing Conditions
Has basic understanding of:
- Sea state in relation to the wind and tide
- Spotting deteriorating weather from visual sky signs
- Tides: springs and neaps; tidal streams, strength, and visual signs
- Choosing a safe sailing location
- Wind awareness

Signature

Sailing Theory
Has an understanding of:
- Sail safe
- The daggerboard: its effect; sailing with/without; all points of sailing
- Centre of Effort and Centre of Lateral Resistance and their effect
- How a sail works

Signature

Equipment
Understands the importance of:
- Board types; uses and limitations
- The relationship between board volume and body weight

- Suitable clothing: accessories and seasonal suitability
- Equipment: purchase, transport, storage, and maintenance

Signature

Other Aspects and Options
Has had an introduction to:
- Windsurfing competition and differing disciplines
- Other aspects – Intermediate Planing Course
- RYA Windsurfing Instructor Courses

Signature

ASSESSMENT CRITERIA

The students should be able to set up their board and rig correctly and suitably for their size and prevailing conditions, enabling them to sail at either a tidal or non-tidal location.

In or above a gentle breeze (seven knots or more), students must be able to launch and recover their equipment, demonstrating an understanding of applying the Fastfwd Formula to tack efficiently; use effective stance on all points of sailing; basic getting-going skills, and harness technique.

The students should show an ability to sail safely and in control, with awareness of hazards in their environment and knowledge of necessary actions to prevent rescue.

Signature

Intermediate Windsurfing: Planing

On completion of the second section of the Intermediate Course you will begin to feel more confident sailing in stronger winds. The course develops knowledge and skills gained, with continuing use of the Formula to be confident in the harness, an essential grounding to getting planing and maintaining blasting control in the footstraps.

It is assumed that any student on this course has mastered the practical skills and background knowledge required for the Intermediate Non-planing Course.

PLANING CRITERIA

Launching, Starting and Landing
Can:

- Carry and launch the board and rig together
- Use improved uphauling in planing conditions
- Stop under control
- Land and come ashore under control

Signature

Sailing Techniques, Stance, and Manoeuvres
Within this section the student should have built a basic practical understanding and be able to apply the Fastfwd Formula ('Vision, Trim, Balance, Power and Stance') to:

- Effectively use the board and sail to encourage planing
- Improve harness technique and line adjustment for the conditions
- Refine stance: for the conditions; on all points of sail
- Cope with gusts and lulls

- Make use of footstraps
- Maintain position in relation to the wind
- Apply basic foot and toe pressure
- Improve steering
- Improve tacking – maintaining speed and flowing movements, and tacking in stronger winds

Signature

Has an understanding of:

- Daggerboard use: sailing with/without; on all points of sailing

Signature

SAILING BACKGROUND

Rigging

Can:

- Rig and de-rig
- Tune equipment suitable to conditions
- Correctly adjust footstraps
- Tie a bowline and a round turn and two half hitches

Signature

Rescue Techniques and Safety

Has an understanding of:

- Towing another board and sailor; tow lines and methods of attachments
- Actions to be taken in potential emergency situations
- Alternative methods of self-rescue

Signature

Sailing Conditions

Has an understanding of:

- Predicting changes in wind direction during a low-pressure system
- Wind and weather associated with a high-pressure system
- Means of recognising dangerous tidal areas
- Choosing a safe sailing venue; weather forecast and tidal information

Signature

Sailing Theory

Understands basic theory on:

- Apparent wind and its effect on the sail as speed changes
- Sailing upwind without a daggerboard
- How a sail works

Signature

Equipment

Has an understanding of:

- The advantages and disadvantages of different types of windsurfing equipment
- Lower volume boards: their uses and limitations
- Board volume in relation to wind strengths
- Types of harness and harness lines available
- Equipment care and storage
- Equipment: purchase, transport, storage, and maintenance

Signature

Other Aspects and Options

Has had an introduction to:

- Windsurfing competition and differing disciplines
- Other Aspects – Advanced and Foiling courses
- RYA Windsurfing Instructor Courses

Signature

ASSESSMENT CRITERIA

The students should be able to set up their board and rig correctly and suitably for their size and prevailing conditions, enabling them to sail at either a tidal or non-tidal location.

In or above a moderate breeze (11 knots plus), students must be able to launch and recover their equipment; demonstrate an understanding of applying the Fastfwd Formula to tack efficiently; show effective stance on all points of sail; demonstrate getting-going technique and use of the harness; understand the beginnings and use of the footstraps, and understand blasting control.

The students should show an ability to sail safely and in control, with awareness of hazards in their environment, showing knowledge of necessary actions to prevent rescue.

Signature

Intermediate Windsurfing: Clinics

ADDITIONAL CLINICS

Beachstarts

An easy-to-master and impressive-looking technique using basic rig and power control, getting both yourself and the rig out on the water and sailing. The core skills and memorable formula established in this clinic form progressive links to the development of the waterstart.

It is assumed that any student on this clinic has mastered a minimum of the practical skills and background knowledge required for the Intermediate Non-planing Windsurfing Course.

PRACTICAL

Sailing Technique

Has a basic understanding of:

- Wind awareness and its effect

Signature

Can:

- Recover the rig
- Control the board and rig together
- Get onto the board in shallow water and sail away using a beachstart
- Beachstart in a variety of wind directions, controlling the board in the shallows

Signature

ASSESSMENT CRITERIA

The students should be able to set up their board and rig correctly and suitably for their size and prevailing conditions, enabling them to sail at either a tidal or non-tidal location.

The students will have built a good level of wind awareness and board/rig control, enabling a confident beachstarting ability in a variety of wind directions and strengths.

The assessment can be completed at either an inland or coastal location.

The students should show an ability to sail safely and in control, with awareness of hazards in their environment, showing knowledge of necessary actions to prevent rescue.

Signature

ADDITIONAL CLINICS

Non-planing Carve Gybe (NPCG)
The first steps towards completing the famous planing carve gybe. On finishing this clinic you will be able to perform a fluid gybe, with footwork and rig control that links directly into a more advanced gybe. The NPCG can be performed in a variety of conditions and can be broken down to aid simplicity and successful learning. It is assumed that any student on this course has mastered the practical skills and background knowledge required for the Intermediate Non-planing Course.

PRACTICAL

Sailing Technique
Has practical understanding and experience of:

- Preparation
- Approach
- Initiation
- Body position
- Rig rotation, timing, and foot change

Signature

Can:
- Complete the non-planing carve gybe

Signature

Has practical understanding of variations in technique to suit conditions:

- Varying gybing exercises
- Sailing clew first
- Maintaining speed and power through the turn

Signature

ASSESSMENT CRITERIA

The students should also be able to set up their board and rig correctly and suitably for their size and prevailing conditions, enabling them to sail at either an inland or coastal location. On completion of the NPCG Clinic, the student will have a confident ability in performing fluid gybes, applying the formula to vary their technique to suit a variety of conditions. The assessment can be completed at either a tidal or non-tidal location. The students should show an ability to sail safely and in control, with awareness of hazards in their environment, showing knowledge of necessary actions to prevent rescue.

Signature

Advanced Windsurfing

On completion of the Advanced Course you will be confident sailing in a variety of wind conditions, on a range of equipment suited to yourself and the environment. Advanced coaching will provide you with improved blasting control on variable water states and confident tacking suitable to the conditions.

Achieving all the skills and knowledge at the Advanced level may take extended coaching and practice time.

It is assumed that any student on this course has mastered the practical skills and background knowledge required for the Intermediate Planing Level.

PRACTICAL

Launching, Starting and Landing
Can:

- Perform controlled launching in a variety of conditions and water states

- Land and position equipment safely ashore

- Uphaul with refinements for lower-volume boards; uses and limitations

Signature

Has awareness of:

- Alternative carrying methods; considering board size; wind strength and direction

Signature

Sailing Techniques, Stance, and Manoeuvres
Has developed an understanding of, and can apply the Fastfwd Formula (Vision, Trim, Balance, Power, Stance) to:

- Get going

- Effectively use the board and sail to encourage early planing

- Achieve blasting control; maintaining control in a variety of conditions including choppy water

- Refine stance according to conditions, on all points of sail; gusts and lulls

- Best use footstraps and harness

Signature

Can tack:

- In stronger winds using improved technique during entry, transition, and exit

- Using differing volume boards suitable to conditions

Signature

SAILING BACKGROUND

Rigging
Can:

- Rig and tune equipment to prevailing conditions

Signature

Rescue Techniques and Safety
Has knowledge of:
- Emergency repairs; action for broken fins, UJs and booms

Understands:
- Different methods of self-help, their uses and limitations
- How to help others in difficulty, with awareness of the situation and how to seek assistance

Sailing Conditions
Has an understanding of:
- Effects of high- and low-pressure systems on wind strength and direction
- Weather created by the passage of warm and cold fronts
- Tidal and wave-driven effects: overfalls; races; rip currents; undertow; dumping waves – causes and effects
- Choosing a suitable sailing location: ideal conditions; tide/weather information

Sailing Theory
Has an understanding of:
- Spin out: causes, effects, and solutions
- Leech twist

Equipment
Has an understanding of:
- Board design – rail shape; rocker; hull and tail shape; volume distribution
- Rigs – type; uses and limitations
- Fins – positioning; shape; design = performance
- Care and maintenance of equipment
- Latest developments in equipment

Other Aspects and Options
- Freestyle
- Foiling courses and equipment

ASSESSMENT CRITERIA

The students should be able to set up their board and rig correctly and suitably for their size and prevailing conditions.

In various conditions and water states, students must be able to launch and recover their equipment; demonstrate an understanding of applying the Fastfwd Formula to tack efficiently; show effective stance on all points of sail, and show advanced getting-going and blasting-control techniques.

Students should show an ability to sail safely and in control, with awareness of other water users, any hazards in their environment, and the knowledge of necessary actions to prevent rescue. All criteria should be assessed on equipment suitable for the conditions.

Assessment is likely to be over a long period, with differing skills being worked upon until competence is demonstrated, at either a tidal or non-tidal location.

Advanced Windsurfing: Clinics

ADDITIONAL CLINICS

Waterstarting

The waterstart is introduced as a means of pulling yourself out of the water when you are at a stage where you wish to move on to lower-volume boards in open water. Pre-mastered fundamentals of rig handling and power control used to complete the waterstart are a progressive link and development from those taught at beachstarting level.

It is assumed that any student on this course has mastered the practical skills and background knowledge required for the Beachstart Clinic.

Has practical understanding and experience of:

- Controlling the board and rig together in deep water

Signature

Can:

- Complete the waterstart
- Vary technique for light and strong winds

Signature

ASSESSMENT CRITERIA

The students should be able to set up their board and rig correctly and suitably for their size and prevailing conditions, enabling them to sail at either a tidal or non-tidal location.

The assessment can be completed at either a tidal or non-tidal location, in conditions in which the students can comfortably plane. Equipment used should be suitable for the prevailing conditions.

The students should show an ability to sail safely and in control, with awareness of hazards in their environment, showing knowledge of necessary actions to prevent rescue.

Signature

ADDITIONAL CLINICS

Planing Carve Gybe

This is the skill every windsurfer throughout their progression aspires to – 'going round corners fast with style'. Having practised and developed the core skills taught during the Non-planing Carve Gybe (NPCG), your Instructor will expand and direct your knowledge towards the end goal of a fluid, controlled turn. During the course you will break down the fundamentals, approaching each section step by step. On completion of this clinic you should be able to use the speed of the board, combined with dynamic weight transfer, to corner successfully with power and grace. It is assumed that any student on this course has mastered the practical skills and background knowledge required for the Advanced Course and Non-planing Carve Gybe Clinic.

PRACTICAL

Sailing Technique
Understands principles of:

- Preparation

- Approach

- Initiation

- Body position

- Rig rotating, timing, and foot change

- Maintaining speed and power through the turn

- Variations in technique to suit conditions

Signature

Can:

- Select and correctly tune equipment to conditions

- Complete the non-planing carve gybe

- Complete the planing carve gybe

Signature

ASSESSMENT CRITERIA

The assessment for the Planing Carve Gybe may need to be carried out over a period of time at either an inland or coastal location, addressing the individual aspects that make up the manoeuvre. The conditions and equipment used should enable the students to plane comfortably.

The students should also be able to set up their board and rig correctly and suitably for their size and prevailing conditions, enabling them to sail at either a tidal or non-tidal location. The students should show an ability to sail safely and in control, with awareness of hazards in their environment, showing knowledge of necessary actions to prevent rescue.

Signature

ADDITIONAL CLINICS

Bump and Jump

The Bump and Jump Clinic is only available at a few specialised centres. It is designed to introduce you to the basic techniques needed to get the board airborne comfortably using a small wave or chop. The clinic will also address progressions in stance and equipment setup in conditions we are likely to be sailing in. As a minimum requirement for this clinic we recommend that you are comfortable sailing hooked in with your feet in both footstraps, have an ability to control suitable equipment in small chop, and are proficiently waterstarting.

To be covered appropriate to location – chop/small waves, in either a tidal or non-tidal environment.

PRACTICAL

Launching, Starting, and Landing
Can:

- Select and tune equipment appropriate to prevailing conditions

- Carry, launch, and recover equipment in small waves/chop

Signature

Sailing Techniques, Stance, and Manoeuvres
Can:

- Refine stance to suit water state

- Sail comfortably in small waves/chop

- Complete basic jumping and landing: preparation; approach; initiation; body position through take-off and landing

Signature

SAILING BACKGROUND

Sailing Theory
Has an understanding of:

- Wind and tide effects

- Shipping forecast interpretation

- Formation of waves: rips; undertows

Signature

Has knowledge of:

- Physical preparation

- Variations of jumping and landing to suit conditions

Signature

ASSESSMENT CRITERIA

The students should be able to set up their board and rig correctly and suitably for their size and prevailing conditions, enabling them to sail at either a tidal or non-tidal location.

The assessment may be carried out over an extended period of time at varying locations and conditions. On completion, the students should be comfortable sailing in a variety of conditions including small waves or chop, and have a basic jumping technique.

The students should show an ability to sail safely and in control, with awareness of hazards in their environment, showing knowledge of necessary actions to prevent rescue.

Signature

ADDITIONAL CLINICS

Advanced Carving Skills

Having mastered the art of carving a board, we can develop this skill and introduce ourselves to a whole new world of carving formations. Using the Fastfwd Formula in a more advanced way, this clinic will help expand your sailing repertoire to an enviable level. It is assumed that any student on this course has mastered the practical skills and background knowledge required for the Advanced Course and Planing Carve Gybe Clinic.

PRACTICAL

Sailing Techniques
Understands the principles of:

- Variations of the carve gybe technique to suit conditions
- Variations in the planing carve gybe: step; strap to strap; duck; slam

Signature

Concentrating on:

- Preparation
- Approach
- Initiation
- Body position
- Rig rotation and foot change
- Maintaining speed and power through the turn

Signature

Can:

- Select and correctly tune equipment to conditions
- Complete the non-planing carve gybe

- Complete the planing carve gybe
- Demonstrate variations in the planing carve gybe: step; strap to strap; duck; slam

Signature

ASSESSMENT CRITERIA

The assessment may be carried out over an extended period of time on suitable equipment at varying locations and conditions either tidal or non-tidal. On completion, the students should be comfortable sailing in a variety of conditions, applying the Formula with the ability to rig and tune appropriate equipment to the conditions, and showing confident variations in carving manoeuvres. The students should show an ability to sail safely and in control, with awareness of hazards in their environment, showing knowledge of necessary actions to prevent rescue.

Signature

RYA WINDFoiling Course: First Flights

The first step in the RYA Windfoil courses, providing you with a basic introduction and initial taster of windfoiling, assisting you to make your first foiling take-off and glides!

By the end of this course you will have an understanding of windfoiling, be able to setup, launch and recover foiling equipment, and make your first short flights on the foil. This short introduction will also provide a basic understanding of the equipment available and opportunities for continuing, including the RYA Sustained Flights Course.

It is assumed that any student on this course has mastered the practical skills and background knowledge at an RYA Intermediate level, and be comfortable blasting in both straps.

Suggested pilot course length/ratio: Two hours 1:1; four hours 1:4 (taster session).

PRACTICAL

Equipment Setup
Understands:

- Foil, board and rig setup
- How to secure a foil safely
- Appropriate footstrap setup
- Rig setup appropriate to conditions

Signature

Launching and Landing
Has knowledge of:

- Foil safety, and uphauling versus waterstarting

Signature

Can:

- Carry foil and board on land
- Launch and recover foils, understanding safe depths

Signature

Sailing Techniques and Manoeuvres
Has knowledge of and understands:

- Using effective pumping technique to get going and encourage flight

Signature

Can:

- Change sailing line and adjust rig position to help initiate flight
- Demonstrate 'take off'

Signature

Understands:

- How to maintain foiling
- How to land in a controlled fashion

Signature

Foiling Knowledge
Has basic understanding of:

- The basic kit setups available

Signature

Safety
Understands:

- The safety requirements of windfoiling and keeping hold of the boom on landing

- The advantages of wearing a helmet

- How RYA Membership provides third-party windsurfing and foiling insurance

Signature

RYA WINDFoiling Course: Sustained Flights

The Sustained Flights Course is designed to increase confidence in foil handling and control, taking you from your first take-offs to sustained flight. Your Instructor will increase your foiling theory background as well as core techniques required to maintain longer glides, and more comfortable flight.

By the end of this course you'll be able to set up and tune your equipment to assist your foiling performance. You will be able to take off, sustain flight, and trim the board effectively, developing the ability to head on different points of sail.

It is assumed that any student on this course has mastered the practical skills and background knowledge at a First Flights and Intermediate level, and is comfortable blasting in both straps.

Suggested course length/ratio: 16 hours or equivalent.

PRACTICAL

Equipment Setup
Can:

- Effectively set up footstrap spread, size and position
- Choose appropriate size sail for conditions

Signature

Understands:

- Foil, board, and rig setup
- Options for changing wing size for the conditions

Signature

Launching and Landing
Can:

- Launch and land confidently

Signature

Understands:

- Changing waterstart technique for foiling, and considering safety aspects of the foil

Signature

Sailing Techniques and Manoeuvres
Can:

- Maintain periods of sustained flight
- Maintain a flat board in foiling
- Trim the sail effectively to the apparent wind to maintain flight
- Use the harness while foiling
- Demonstrate good foiling stance
- Use effective board and rig pumping if needed to encourage flight.

- Demonstrate basic steering towards and away from the wind while foiling
- Land in a controlled manner

Signature

Understands:

- How to steer and maintain foiling upwind for tack entry
- How to steer and maintain foiling downwind for gybe entry

Signature

Can:

- Perform a non-foiling tack
- Perform a non-foiling gybe

Signature

Foiling Knowledge
Understands:

- How apparent wind affects flight and sailing position.

Signature

Has Knowledge of:

- The advantages and disadvantages of different mast and fuselage lengths
- High- and low-aspect wings

Signature

Safety
Has knowledge and awareness of:

- The lack of noise when approaching other craft
- The angles foiling craft sail compared with traditional non-foiling craft

Signature

RYA WINDFoiling Course: Performance Flights

Performance Flights looks to take you from the skills and techniques acquired in Sustained Flights to controlling the foil with confidence in a wider range of conditions and sailing angles.

You will be entering transitions on the foil, as well as building the skills and knowledge to complete foiling gybes.

By the end of this course you should have the knowledge and skills to be able to foil comfortably on all points of sail, sustaining flight into tacks and gybes. You will also have the knowledge and understanding for foiling gybe entry, mid, and exits, if full foiling gybes have not been achieved during the course.

It is assumed that any student on this course has mastered the practical skills and background knowledge required, and is at the level of Sustained Flights.

Suggested course length: 16 hours or equivalent.

PRACTICAL

Equipment Setup
Can:

- Set up foil wing size and angles for prevailing conditions

- Understand the adjustment of footstrap setup to aid gybing on the foil

- Adjust mastfoot position for prevailing conditions and foil setup

- Tune the sail to promote foiling and effective control

- Understand the best types of rigs for better performance when foiling

Signature

Sailing Techniques and Manoeuvres
Can:

- Demonstrate good foiling stance on all points of sail in a variety of water states

- Demonstrate effective steering into a tack

- Complete a tack with a foiling entry and controlled exit

- Demonstrate effective steering into a gybe

- Demonstrate gybe entry while foiling

- Complete a gybe with a foiling entry and controlled exit (non-foiling)

Signature

Understands:

- How to maintain control when overpowered
- The correct rig, body, and footwork adjustments required to foil through a gybe

Safety

- Has an awareness of safety during foiling transitions
- Has knowledge of personal safety equipment which may be worn while foiling

Signature

Signature

RYA Racing Course
Start Racing

Racing Background

Racing Pathways and Structure
Has knowledge of:

- Club and local racing

- Scheme structure

- Equipment used in club and regional racing

RACING THEORY

Racing Knowledge
Has an understanding of:

- A racing start line

- The port/starboard rule

- A simple starting sequence

- Being close to the start line on the gun

- Wind shadows

- The legs of a course, i.e. beat, reach, run

Signature

Wind/Weather/Tide
Can:

- Obtain and understand a simple weather forecast

- Select the correct rig and equipment for the conditions

- Understand high and low tide

Signature

PRE-RACE PREPARATION

Equipment Preparation
Has an understanding of:

- Boom height

- How to prevent boom slippage

- Tightening battens

- Setting a sail for the conditions

Signature

Board and Kit Care
Can:

- Carry out a visual inspection (looking for cracks, holes)

- Avoid damage, stones, and rough surfaces

Signature

Health and Nutrition
Has knowledge of:

- Food as a fuel

- Keeping hydrated

Signature

Fitness
Has knowledge of:

- The physical demands of racing

- Performing basic injury prevention, i.e. warm up, cool down, stretching

Signature

TECHNIQUE

Starting
Can demonstrate the basics of:

- Getting near the start line on the gun

- Stopping and holding position

Speed
Can demonstrate the basics of:

- Developing stance

- Trimming the board upwind and downwind

Can demonstrate the basics of:

- Faster tacks and gybes

- Gybing around a mark, entering wide and exiting tight

Can demonstrate the basics of:

- Keeping clear wind

- Tacking in the correct place for windward marks

Once you have completed Start Racing, you should be able to race around a course in a small fleet and understand the starting procedure and course configuration.

> **!** **TAKE A CHALLENGE**
> **Take part in local club racing**

Intermediate Racing

RACING BACKGROUND

Racing Pathways and Structure
Has knowledge of:
- Regional and national race structures
- Equipment used in international and national racing
- UKWA regional racing
- The role of the RYA and UKWA

Signature

RACING THEORY

Racing Knowledge
Has an understanding of:
- Racing courses
- The windward/leeward rule
- A standard starting sequence, including flags
- Being on the start line on the gun
- Taking penalties (360°)
- Hailing protest
- Clear air and positioning at the start

Signature

Wind/Weather/Tide
Can:
- Obtain, understand, and use a weather forecast
- Select the correct settings for the conditions
- Understand tides and timings of high and low water
- Spot and react to gusts

Signature

PRE-RACE PREPARATION

Equipment Preparation
Has an understanding of:
- Rig settings for different conditions
- When to change up/down sail size
- Adjustable harness lines and setting the lines in the correct position
- Legal sail numbers and positioning

Signature

Board and Kit Care
Can:
- Ensure the daggerboard works easily and effectively
- Keep the fin and daggerboard in good condition

Signature

Health and Nutrition
Has an understanding of:
- Using food to enhance performance
- The effects of dehydration

Signature

Fitness
Has knowledge of:
- The requirement for physical fitness and training for racing
- The regular use of injury-prevention techniques, warm up/cool down and stretching

Signature

TECHNIQUE

Starting
Can demonstrate the basics of:
- Practice reversing
- Controlling the board in tight situations
- Manoeuvring under control

Signature

Speed
Can demonstrate the basics of:
- Achieving the correct pointing angle
- Using railing upwind
- Rapid and efficient daggerboard movement relative to leg
- Using the harness
- Beginning to develop pumping technique

Signature

Turning Techniques
Can demonstrate the basics of:
- Faster gybing in stronger winds
- Accelerating out of tacks and resuming pointing angle

Signature

Tactics and Strategy
Has knowledge and understanding of:
- Leeward mark roundings
- Deciding which side of the beat to go up, and awareness that the two sides may not be equal
- Spotting and using wind shifts on the upwind leg

Signature

The knowledge and practical experience gained by completing the Intermediate Racing Certificate should enable you to race around a course and make race decisions based upon rules and strategy, with an awareness of other competitors.

> **TAKE A CHALLENGE**
> **Attend UKWA regional race events**

Advanced Racing

RACING BACKGROUND

Racing Pathways and Structure
Has knowledge of:

- UK racing structure/class associations and equipment

- Class rules

- National racing

RACING THEORY

Racing Knowledge
Has an understanding of:

- The use of racing courses

- The basics of RRS (Racing Rules of Sailing) part 1

- The basics of RRS part 2

Wind/Weather/Tide
Can:

- Understand and show awareness of the sea-breeze effect

- Predict conditions from simple weather forecasts

- Demonstrate an awareness of the relevance and effect of tidal streams

PRE-RACE PREPARATION

Equipment Preparation
Has an understanding of:

- Rig settings using adjustable outhaul and downhaul

- How to set a sail for maximum performance in all conditions

- Essential spares for competition

- Ensuring equipment is class legal and complies with current class rules

Board and Kit Care
Can:

- Maintain foils and hull in a good condition

- Demonstrate knowledge of basic board repair

Health and Nutrition
Has an understanding of:

- The use of sports drinks

- The effective use of food as a performance enhancer

Fitness
Has knowledge of:

- Establishing a basic fitness regime for windsurfing

- Incorporating body-weight training into a fitness programme

TECHNIQUE

Starting
Can demonstrate the basics of:

- Developing a starting plan

- Creating gaps on the start line using board control

- Accelerating and predicting the gun to ensure speed at the start

Signature

Speed
Can demonstrate the basics of:

- Using a tuning partner to test speed and height upwind

- Keeping a constant and smooth angle upwind

- Mast track adjustment

- Solid pumping technique both up and downwind

- Effective stance and control downwind

Signature

Turning Techniques
Can demonstrate the basics of:

- Carve gybing

- Faster 360° penalty turns

Signature

Tactics and Strategy
Has knowledge and understanding of:

- Pre-race planning, checking the course and making a decision as to which way to go

- Recognition and awareness of wind shifts

- Bearing away in a gust downwind

Signature

An Advanced Racing certificate means you have the skills to prepare yourself for a race around a course in a large fleet and make decisions, using rules, tactics, and strategy, both in regard to your own sailing and that of the fleet.

> ! **TAKE A CHALLENGE**
> Take part in UKWA national events

Becoming an Instructor

If you have enjoyed your experiences of learning to windsurf and developing your techniques and skills through the RYA Windsurfing Scheme, why not consider sharing your enthusiasm, expertise, and skills with others by becoming involved in the RYA Instructor Training programme?

Below are brief details concerning the basic training courses. More information can be found in W33 RYA Windsurfing Instructor Manual.

RYA ASSISTANT INSTRUCTOR

Duration: Two days/20 hours

Role
The RYA Assistant Instructor is trained to assist qualified Instructors to teach beginners on the Start Windsurfing course of the RYA Windsurfing Scheme and the RYA Youth Windsurfing Scheme Stage 2. They must only work under the supervision of a Senior Instructor. The award is centre-specific.

Eligibility for the Training Course
An Assistant Instructor is a competent windsurfer holding the minimum of Intermediate Non-planing Personal Certificate. They are not required to use a powerboat unless they hold the RYA Powerboat Level 2 Certificate.

Training
Training will cover the centre's safe-operation procedures and the teaching points related to teaching beginners. The award is centre-specific. Training is based on a two-day or modular course of 20 hours' duration at the centre run by the Principal/ Chief Instructor who holds a valid RYA Senior Instructor certificate.

Assessment
Candidates will be assessed on their practical teaching ability with beginners. Successful candidates will be awarded an RYA Assistant Instructor certificate by their Principal.

RYA START WINDSURFING INSTRUCTOR

Duration: Five days/50 hours

Role

A Start Windsurfing Instructor is a competent windsurfer trained to teach and assess the Start Windsurfing syllabus, and Stage 1 and 2 of the Youth Scheme. Start Windsurfing Instructors are confident windsurfers capable of teaching the basic skills of windsurfing in light to medium winds, under the supervision of an RYA Senior Instructor.

Eligibility for the Training Course

- Minimum age 16
- Valid first aid certificate (see www.rya.org.uk/go/firstaidcertificates)
- RYA Powerboat Level 2 certificate
- RYA Safe & Fun
- RYA Intermediate Non-planing Personal Certificate, or sailing assessment completed
- RYA membership

During the course a sailing assessment may be carried out covering the basic skills and techniques an Instructor would be expected to show, such as stopping and starting under control, turning on the spot, tacking, and gybing. Passing this assessment is a requirement of the qualification.

Training

The structure and content of the RYA Windsurfing Scheme and the RYA Youth Windsurfing Scheme; training in the RYA teaching methods for both adults and children; the assessment of students' abilities, and the use of a powered craft in a teaching environment.

Assessment

The Start Windsurfing course runs over five days, with the final day moderated by an external trainer who has not been involved in or associated with the training course. The assessment will be based on an overall judgement throughout the week and during the moderation day, in areas such as enthusiasm for the sport; sailing ability; confidence and knowledge in the sport; awareness of safety, and knowledge and practical application of the RYA teaching method.

During the moderation, candidates may be required to demonstrate confident ability in areas such as delivery of on- and off-water sessions; preparation; management and structure of sessions; theoretical knowledge, and windsurfing ability.

PLEASE ATTACH
YOUR RYA CERTIFICATE
HERE

**Please note that no record
of certificates is held by the RYA**

**Enquiries about lost certificates
should be made to the centre
where the course was taken**

PLEASE ATTACH YOUR RYA CERTIFICATE HERE

Please note that no record of certificates is held by the RYA

Enquiries about lost certificates should be made to the centre where the course was taken

PLEASE ATTACH YOUR RYA CERTIFICATE HERE

Please note that no record of certificates is held by the RYA

Enquiries about lost certificates should be made to the centre where the course was taken

PLEASE ATTACH
YOUR RYA CERTIFICATE
HERE

**Please note that no record
of certificates is held by the RYA**

**Enquiries about lost certificates
should be made to the centre
where the course was taken**

PLEASE ATTACH
YOUR RYA CERTIFICATE
HERE

**Please note that no record
of certificates is held by the RYA**

**Enquiries about lost certificates
should be made to the centre
where the course was taken**